PREPARING AND PRESENTING YOUR ARBITRATION CASE

PREPARING AND PRESENTING YOUR ARBITRATION CASE

A Manual for Union and Management Representatives

Allan J. Harrison

Institute of Labor and Industrial Relations
University of Illinois at Urbana-Champaign

THE BUREAU OF NATIONAL AFFAIRS, INC., Washington, D.C. 20037

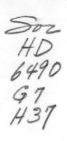

Library of Congress Cataloging in Publication Data

Harrison, Allan J
  Preparing and presenting your arbitration case.

  1. Grievance arbitration—Handbooks, manuals, etc.
I. Title
HD6490.G7H37   658.31'54   79-10189
ISBN 0-87179-303-2

International Standard Book Number: 0-87179-303-2
Printed in the United States of America

Contents

1

Introduction

Purpose

The following manual, a compilation of materials and ideas taken from many sources, is designed to train union and management representatives to better prepare and present grievance arbitration cases. Moreover, as a workbook, it reflects an approach to arbitration which emphasizes the *preparation* of evidence and arguments by the parties prior to the arbitration hearing and minimizes the importance of formality and legalism in the *presentation* of the arbitration case.

The organization of the material attempts to parallel the normal chronological order in which a given grievance develops into an arbitration case. Obviously, many questions occur repeatedly as a grievance proceeds to resolution, but in this manual such questions will seldom be dealt with more than once. The table of contents and some cross-referencing should be sufficient to allow the reader to keep track of such recurring questions and permit him to follow the manual as he prepares his case.

Grievance Arbitration and Arbitrators

In the United States the most accepted method of resolving disputes arising under a labor agreement is arbitration. Well over 90 percent of the labor agreements designate arbitration as the final step in their grievance procedure.

Labor arbitrators are impartial third parties, with no self-interest in the resolution of the disputes they are selected to hear and decide. Although they bring to the dispute their own knowledge, background, and skills, they are truly creatures of the two parties, with their powers usually specifically limited to the interpretation and application of the particular agreement under which a given grievance has arisen.

All of us, including arbitrators, recognize that many grievances are taken up and resolved by the parties in a manner that may not be in strict conformity with the written labor agreement. However, arbitrators do not have the same powers as the two parties, who have considerable latitude in mutually adding to or altering an agreement.

In view of these inherent limitations in the arbitral process, the following material will emphasize the importance of contract language in preparing grievances for arbitration. Other matters, such as "fairness" or "efficiency," which may sometimes prove persuasive in the grievance procedure, will receive much less emphasis in this manual.

Grievance Arbitration, Fact-Finding, Mediation, etc.

Grievance arbitration is sometimes referred to as "rights arbitration" in that the arbitrator makes a decision concerning the "rights" of the parties under an existing labor agreement. The arbitration of issues at impasse in contract negotiations, on the other hand, is often called "interest arbitration," because the arbitator is being asked to determine how the interests of the parties should be incorporated into a new labor agreement. The latter form of labor arbitration is relatively rare in this country and finds its most common use in public-sector bargaining. Usually in the public sector the neutral third party makes only non-binding recommendations for a settlement and is often called an "advisory arbitrator" or a "fact finder."

Perhaps the most common form of neutral third-party involvement in labor relations is mediation during contract negotiations. In mediation, the mediator or conciliator normally makes no public recommendations or even public statements concerning the proper resolution of the issues in dispute. He (or she) is there to facilitate the process of collective bargaining and not to make decisions about the terms of any new agreement.

2

The Grievance Procedure

One must always keep in mind that arbitration is simply the last step of the grievance procedure—a step that should rarely be taken if the grievance procedure has been effective. One hopes that in the course of the grievance procedure the parties will reach an agreement that disposes of the grievance. To that purpose, a grievance procedure allows for review of a dispute by those union and company representatives who should be able to judge a case more objectively than the supervisor and employee(s) immediately involved. Furthermore, the procedure allows both parties time to obtain the facts needed to fully understand a case. Both parties hope that the increased objectivity and information will combine to produce a resolution of the dispute. Even if they do not, they should make clear to the parties what their differences are; what exactly each is contending; and upon what evidence their respective cases are based. In short, before going to arbitration, the parties should have thoroughly discussed their differences and should clearly understand one another's contentions. There should be no surprises at the arbitration hearing.

Definition of a Grievance or Scope of the Procedure

Many grievance procedures permit the processing of all sorts of employee complaints which may not have any basis in contract language. This practice is often the effect of broadly defining a grievance, and it results in employees feeling free to make claims that the union cannot satisfy in arbitration. Typically the arbitration provisions constrain the arbitrator to the interpretation and application of the labor agreement. In these circumstances, union leadership has a continual task of explaining that, although a matter is grievable, it does not necessarily mean the case can be arbitrated successfully, or at all.

Management, too, must consider the consequences of broadly defining grievances; and it is a rare employer who does not prefer a clearly circumscribed definition of a grievance. Whether working within a contract that broadly or narrowly defines grievances, however, most companies in the interests of labor peace should entertain or discuss matters of employee concern, even though they may not meet the contract's definition of a grievance. At the same time, when management does discuss employee complaints which it believes are not true "grievances" under the contract, it should make that position clear from the outset.

Time Limits

From both union and company standpoints it is also important to recognize that there are time limits for appealing grievances at each step of the procedure. If these limits are not met by the union, it generally results in the grievance being settled on the basis of the last employer answer.

In this connection, unions would do well to keep in mind that delay works against the union in almost all cases. First, to many employees, justice delayed is justice denied; receiving four hours back pay in July may not satisfy the grievant who expected that "report-in-pay" the week before Christmas. Time has eroded the meaning of the remedy. Second, the typical grievance occurs after management has taken some action. While the grievance wanders through the grievance procedure, management's decision stands. Moreover, seldom does a decision result in a retroactive cost to the employer; more rarely still is that retroactive cost any greater to the employer than if he had initially complied with the contract. Even when there might be a back-pay award, it would be better for the union to have the situation rectified early rather than to wait, perhaps a year, for a remedy which makes the employee whole for his loss.

Most contracts, of course, have clear time limits which would move a grievance through in a relatively brief time if both parties adhered to those limits. Unfortunately unions often cooperate in, and even request, the extension of those time limits. Needless to say, there are many reasons why unions wish to delay the processing of a given grievance. In some cases the union simply needs more time to obtain facts or to decide whether the case has merit. In other instances it may be hoping that the problem will go away; the company will give in and put the man back to work after a month; the grievant will quit, retire, or die. Whatever the reason, delay not only works against the union for all the reasons stated above, but it also projects a poor union image to its membership. Moreover, it may lull a union into situations where it fails to appeal a case properly, thereby making the grievance nonarbitrable.

On the other hand, it is difficult to believe, in spite of the foregoing, that the employer's interest, on the whole, is advanced by unwarranted delay in the processing of grievances. Plainly there are numerous instances when the delay does benefit management, but an employer who pursues a policy of deliberate delay must ultimately expect to pay for that policy in employee discontent and bad relations with the union.

The employer does, however, have the right to expect a union to timely file grievances and to pursue those grievances in accordance with the grievance procedure. It is not being unreasonably technical when it insists that the union do so. The employer should, of course, try to be consistent in this respect, thus insuring against sloppy procedures developing gradually.

Role of Representatives

Another important procedural aspect is representation: Who acts as the representative at each step, and what is the extent of an individual's right to process his own grievances? The NLRA permits individual employees to process a grievance without union interference, provided that any adjustment of that grievance conforms to the labor agreement and a union representative has the opportunity to be present at such adjustment.

Ideally, under a negotiated grievance procedure, the union representative would have the right to be present at all discussions of grievances whether those discussions result in adjustment or not. This would insure against both favoritism and an individual agreement's undercutting the contract. Unfortunately, unions often fail to keep track of what is going on due to lack of interest, timidity, or just plain laziness.

It should be added that many companies and some unions follow a deliberate policy of encouraging employees and supervisors to resolve problems without union involvement. Some managements believe that opportunities for adjustment are increased when disputes are at an informal stage, and that formal union involvement tends to freeze the position of the parties. Some unions tend to agree and encourage such informal resolution.

Management may sometimes pursue such a policy, however, simply to exclude and weaken the union. A policy pursued for those purposes can result in a number of consequences which normally are not desired by management. There are obviously potential NLRA violations. Even more important than legal consequences are the dangers of increased favoritism and the growth of non-contractual, surreptitious employment practices which are successfully concealed, not only from the union, but from middle and upper management as well.

The contract may specify who handles the grievances at various steps, whose signatures must be placed on the grievance, whether or not the union may file a grievance on behalf of the union as a whole, etc. Whatever the specifications, the parties should adhere to these contractual requirements, keeping in mind that failure to do so, and the growth of slipshod practices, must inevitably rebound against both.

Powers and Payment of Arbitrators

The arbitration provision usually makes clear the powers, the method of selection, and the payment of the arbitrator. It is rare indeed that the arbitrator's powers extend beyond the interpretation and application of the labor agreement. Selection procedures vary (see Chapter 4, "Selection of Arbitrator"). Payment methods also vary. Although shared equal payment of the arbitrator is the rule, there is at least one variation worth discussing, if not worth adopting.

"Loser pay" clauses provide that the party who loses the case must pay the arbitrator. Aside from the difficulty of collecton that this may place on the arbitrator, this is usually a losing proposition from a union's standpoint. Most unions take more close cases (or downright losers) to arbitration simply because union representatives, to a much greater degree than management, must satisfy a political constituency.

Moreover, there is a difficulty for both labor and management in that many cases are not clearcut losses for anyone, e.g., the discharged employee who is reinstated without back pay. How, then, should that bill be divided?

Finally, for both parties the "loser pay" concept introduces an element of gamesmanship to the selection of cases for arbitration which is not in accord with a process of encouraging the parties to reason with one another over their problems. Gamesmanship assumes a competitive system, not a working cooperative process which exists to resolve problems rather than to keep score.

Improving Arbitration Clauses

Arbitration clauses are also the appropriate contractual area for the parties to remedy some of the problems and complaints they have about the process.

Parties sometimes complain that they are forced into the position of either paying for a transcript or being at a disadvantage in the submission of post-hearing arguments or briefs. Although much contract language could be suggested, a simple sentence stating that "written transcripts will be made of the arbitration hearing only with the mutual consent of the parties" would be effective. This would give each party a veto over the use of court reporters but leave them free to use one should both agree that a transcript is warranted.

The same type of language would prevent one representative from always submitting, and putting the other side's representative to the task of submitting, unnecessary post-hearing briefs. A sentence stating "post-hearing briefs will only be permitted when both parties agree to file such briefs" would control this problem.

Certainly it is in both parties' interests to operate as informally and expeditiously as possible. Although labor lawyers bring many skills to the arbitration process, the increasing legalism of arbitration, and the attendant legalistic paraphernalia of transcripts and briefs, does not do a service for the parties or the process. In spite of all their well-publicized difficulties, perhaps the United Mine Workers of America and the Bituminous Coal Operators Association are on to something. They have for years agreed in their grievance procedure that:

"Neither party will be represented by an attorney licensed to practice law in any jurisdiction in any of the steps of the grievance procedure except by mutual agreement applicable only to a particular case." National Bituminous Coal Wage Agreement.

3

Procedural and Substantive Arbitrability

A question of arbitrability is essentially a claim that an issue cannot properly be decided by an arbitrator. Nearly always, this claim is made by an employer. There are two distinctly different kinds of claims, generally referred to as procedural and substantive arbitrability questions.

A procedural challenge to arbitrability is usually an allegation that the union has failed to follow the grievance procedure properly. For example, a company might claim that the union failed to appeal the grievance from the first to the second step of the procedure within the contractually established time limits. Or, in another instance, an employer might contend that the union is attempting to arbitrate two issues when the contract limits arbitation to only one issue at a time.

A claim that a matter is not substantively arbitrable is a claim that the subject matter, or substance, of the grievance itself cannot be an issue for an arbitrator to decide. Suppose a union grieved the promotion of a certain individual to plant superintendent. The company might contend that this matter is not arbitrable since the substance of the grievance deals with internal management policy, a subject clearly not covered by the labor agreement. Or a company might contest the arbitrability of any grievance protesting its marketing or finance policies, since these matters are rarely covered by labor agreements. In short, a substantive arbitrability question is a challenge that the nature of the grievance does not fall within the negotiated contractual relationship, and therefore an arbitrator has no authority to resolve the issue.

When a company refuses to submit a case to arbitration on the claim that it is nonarbitrable, for either procedural or substantive reasons, a union may ultimately have to take the matter to federal district court to obtain arbitration. However, companies will agree, in many instances, to allow an arbitrator to determine whether the grievance is arbitrable.

It is an unfortunate and unfair fact of life that under most labor agreements there is no completely satisfactory way of dealing with employers who abuse the claims of nonarbitrability, and who thereby not only force a union into unnecessary legal and arbitral expense but also cause unwarranted delay in the resolution of grievances. However, the federal law does insure that a grievance may be heard when the company's claim of nonarbitrability lacks merit.

In cases where the company claims a grievance is procedurally not arbitrable, the Supreme Court has ruled that such procedural issues must be left to the arbitrator to decide. Most employers will agree to have an arbitrator decide this matter, although it may prove necessary to have a federal district court direct the company to submit the matter to arbitration. Still, under federal laws the question of procedural arbitrability itself is not a matter to be litigated in the courts.

On the other hand, if the company argues that a matter is substantively not arbitrable, and refuses to allow an arbitrator to decide the issue, the union's only recourse is to take the issue into federal district court; that is, the parties must argue whether or not the issue is arbitrable before the court, and the district court will resolve the question. To further confuse events, a federal district court may, in some instances, direct that the matter be submitted to an arbitrator and will not itself decide the issue of arbitrability.

At this point union representatives can readily appreciate that a question of arbitrability causes both increased delay and greater costs. In addition to these rather obvious burdens, an employer's tactical use of questions of arbitrability may also prejudice the outcome of the arbitration case.

When both the arbitrability and the merits are heard by the same arbitrator, there is a danger he may "split" his award, i.e., give the arbitrability question to the union but the merits to the company. That's the only way such a dual decision can be split. (If the arbitrability is denied, the merits are not considered.) Such a half loaf, as a practical matter, is half of nothing as far as the union is concerned.

Even more insidious is the danger that a claim of substantive nonarbitrability will strongly suggest to the arbitrator that the grievance itself can have no merit. If a case, according to one party, is not even covered by the labor agreement, how can the labor agreement possibly have been violated? Once this idea is planted in the mind of an arbitrator, it can be a difficult presumption for a union to overcome.

What can be done by unions to counter the frivolous and tactical use of claims of nonarbitrability? In cases of both procedural and substantive arbitrability, a union can propose that both the arbitrability and the merits be submitted to the arbitrator and then hope to avoid "splitters." If the company refuses, the union can ask the district court to direct arbitration if the arbitrability issue is only procedural. In a case of substantive arbitrability the union would usually be better off to ask the district court to resolve the matter without further ado, rather than add more cost and delay by returning it to an arbitrator.

If both the arbitrability and merits are to be decided by one arbitrator, the union should be prepared to demonstrate to the arbitrator that the company has raised the question as a "tactic," if such is indeed the case. For example, if the company has often raised arbitrability questions in previous cases, point this out to the arbitrator.

The best union solution to procedural arbitrability problems, of course, is to make sure that stewards and local officers always follow the procedure exactly. If they can't, a union should try to negotiate a procedure they can follow.

In the case of substantive arbitrability problems, a union might consider changing the grievance procedure to clearly permit a strike over any dispute an employer claims is nonarbitrable. This raises some real problems where the membership is seeking every opportunity to strike, and should obviously only be considered after much provocation. Under such circumstances a company would, in most cases, lose any interest it might have in raising such questions for tactical reasons. Such an exception to the no-strike provision would, however, not make much sense in the case of procedural arbitrability issues. Stewards and local officers would be tempted, in certain instances, deliberately not to follow the grievance procedure in order that a given grievance might occasion a strike. It is also true that procedural arbitrability questions normally result in much less delay; frivolous claims can usually be recognized as frivolous; and, in any event, such claims do not require the lengthy litigation often involved in issues of substantive arbitrability.

In short, since the union is almost always the grieving party, questions of arbitrability are often a considerable burden. No easy answer to this problem exists, and only a good relationship can prevent an employer's tactical abuse of what are, normally, quite legitimate claims.*

There are, of course, numerous instances when a company is completely justified in its refusal to arbitrate a matter on either procedural or substantive grounds. But companies must take care not to damage their justifiable claims. Continually allowing the union to be lax in following the grievance procedure or repeatedly failing to raise either a procedural or substantive objection in a timely and prompt fashion not only seriously undercuts the employer's objections, but may even suggest that his claim of nonarbitrability is frivolous. Moreover, when the employer is as lax as the union in following the grievance

---

*Public sector unions, not covered by the NLRA, face questions of arbitrability which often must be resolved by state courts interpreting state laws. Needless to say, the states vary considerably on such matters.

procedure, its moral position is discredited although its contractual stance may still have merit.

Many problems of substantive arbitrability arise from a failure by both parties to insist on concise language at the bargaining table. This writer is not enamored with elaborate management rights clauses or boilerplate zipper clauses (although the latter certainly have uses); rather he is convinced that the parties should work out the scope of their agreement on all matters of concern at the bargaining table and should not use boilerplate as a substitute for thought, nor should they need the courts to define those limits.

Finally, unions sometimes abuse grievance procedures for political ends as well as in an effort to gain concessions not agreed to in the bargaining process. Furthermore, it is not unusual for a company to see advantages in ignoring or evading the contractual procedures and in reaching extra-contractual understandings. But such wheeling-dealing is apt to get out of hand. A company and a union that insist on following the established procedures and settling matters based on the written contract are not likely to lose control of their labor relations based on informal and undefined "understandings."

4

Selection of Arbitrator

Various Contractual Methods

Generally the labor agreement stipulates the way in which an arbitrator will be selected, and no one method is necessarily superior to any other. For unions and companies which seldom take a grievance to arbitration, it probably makes most sense to have a method of selecting an "ad hoc" arbitrator, that is, an arbitrator for each case. If the parties cannot agree on an arbitrator, the American Arbitration Association or the Federal Mediation and Conciliation Service can provide assistance. They provide lists or "panels" of five or seven names, and the two parties then number or strike names until the "least undesirable" arbitrator is chosen. There is a modest charge by the AAA for this service, but the AAA also takes care of all the scheduling details. The FMCS simply appoints the selected arbitrator and leaves it to him and the parties to find a commonly acceptable date, time, and place for a hearing.

For unions and companies that take many cases to arbitration, it may be desirable to establish some form of umpire system that assures a prompt hearing from a mutually acceptable arbitrator. Umpire systems vary somewhat, and range from using a single umpire to having several arbitrators who take cases in turn.

Many contracts also call for tripartite boards consisting of a union representative, a company representative, and a neutral. It is difficult to see how the cumbersome and usually time-consuming nature of such tripartite systems has any compensating advantages. It can be argued, though, that in specific instances and specific industries such boards act as a check on the ignorance of the outside arbitrator. Still, one wonders how two additional advocates can enlighten an arbitrator outside the hearing, if the two parties have failed to do so during the hearing. Moreover, the time spent obtaining input from two other people when preparing an award must only increase the cost and the time of obtaining that award. Furthermore, when the company and union members of a panel begin to "concur in part" and "dissent in part" from the neutral's decision, complete confusion can take place regarding the actual "majority opinion." It is probably significant that in practice many tripartite panels established in labor agreements are regularly ignored by the parties.

Finding out About an Arbitrator

Whether you are choosing an arbitrator to act as a permanent panel member or merely to hear one case, there is really a very limited information system to aid in your selection.

The Bureau of National Affairs, Inc., and Commerce Clearing House, Inc., regularly publish arbitrators' decisions, and it is possible to find and read a number of decisions by most practicing arbitrators. However, one must keep in mind that BNA and CCH do not publish all decisions mailed to them, and arbitrators often are not permitted by one, or both, of the parties to submit a decision for publication. Then again, arbitrators themselves do not always choose to submit a decision for publication. It is not in an arbitrator's interest to have a poorly or hurriedly written decision published. Therefore, when reading an arbitrator's published decisions, one must realize that they represent only a narrow portion of his output, and possibly only the portion he considers most helpful to his reputation. As a particular arbitrator's published decisions may also be unrelated to the issue you are facing, the only purpose usually served by reading those decisions is a slight familiarity with his style and approach to problems.

Additional useful information may often be obtained by checking with other parties who have dealt with the arbitrator often, such as on an umpire basis, and, consequently, have experienced his work over a range of cases and situations. A call to your counterpart in the other company or union will prove quite helpful if he has indeed had considerable experience with the arbitrator in question and is willing to level with you.

5

Preparing the Case

Contract Language as the Point of Departure

When preparing a case, the central questions are whether or not the employer violated the contract language and what, if anything, is the appropriate remedy for that violation? If no provision has been violated, it will be almost impossible for an arbitrator to award in favor of the union. And, if no remedy is available for the violation, the union is probably wasting its own and the company's money on arbitration.

In the rare case of a contract which permits grievances by the company against the union, the above questions should be altered accordingly. However, any contractual terms binding on the union, such as "no strike" clauses, are typically enforced in courts and not through the grievance and arbitral provisions.

Labor and management representatives, then, must spend considerable time reading pertinent contract language and determining how best to establish that there was or was not a violation of that language and what, if anything, is an appropriate remedy.

The evidence needed to support a case will be dictated by the particular provision(s) the union contends has (have) been violated. It is senseless for either party to collect facts that are irrelevant to an alleged violation, no matter what else they may illustrate about the company and the union or employees. Without becoming bogged down in a mass of superfluous information, one must be sure that all the evidence, arguments, and joint stipulations (testimony and exhibits) are directed at establishing or disproving two crucial contentions: The employer did violate one or more provisions of the contract language; the union and/or employee is entitled to a remedy.

Once collected, the evidence may suggest more than one approach to the case. A representative may then decide to select the strongest of these approaches for which there is supporting evidence. Or, he may choose to present a few different approaches and the related evidence to the arbitrator as alternatives from which the arbitrator is urged to choose. A single theory has the disadvantage that it may not be persuasive and the arbitrator may then have no alternative but to rule in favor of your adversary. On the other hand, the presentation of several theories may reduce the power of any single argument and may moreover lead to confusion and conflict within one's presentation.

No matter what his final approach, however, a representative's case preparation should always begin with a study of the contract language. The following information is intended to familiarize the representative with some of the more commonly accepted standards for interpreting language in controversy.*

Language Which Is Clear and Unambiguous

Although the parties may attempt to place a forced interpretation on a given provision, contract language is often relatively clear and unambiguous to the neutral reader. The following are examples of contract language and possible interpretations. Is the language clear and unambiguous?

Example 1: "The company will provide required safety equipment."

The company argues this merely means that it must make equipment available for employee purchase. The union contends the company has agreed to pay for the equipment.

Example 2: "The senior qualified bidder will be awarded the position."

The company argues that the senior employee must be able to perform the work without training. The union contends that the employee need only be able to learn the job in a reasonable time period.

Example 3: "An employee must work on the schedule day before and after the holiday in order to receive holiday pay."

The union argues that employees need not work a full shift prior to and after

---

*This material is based in part on a section of Elkouri & Elkouri, *How Arbitration Works*, 3rd ed. (Washington, D.C.: BNA Books, 1973), pp. 296-320.

the holiday, as long as they work some portion of those scheduled days. The company argues that the contract requires the employee to work a full shift the scheduled day before and after.

Specific Versus General Language

Specific contract language will be given the arbitrator's consideration over more general provisions. The parties are presumed to have examined the matter more closely when specific and detailed language is negotiated and, consequently, defined their more general intentions by that specific language.

Example 1: "The company shall continue to make reasonable provisions for the safety and health of its employees."

"Wearing apparel and other equipment necessary to protect employees from injury shall be provided by the company in accordance with practices now prevailing or as such practices may be improved from time to time by the company."

How would you guess an arbitrator would rule on a case asking that rain clothes be provided outside employees, if this had not been done before?

Example 2: "Senior employees will be given first choice among vacation periods."

"Members of the maintenance department will have a choice of vacation periods based on seniority to the degree possible; so long as there is an adequate maintenance crew for the efficient conduct of the employer's business."

The three maintenance electricians all request vacation for the same time. The company denies the vacation period to the junior of the three and instead permits a still more junior maintenance pipe fitter to take vacation. The union asks that the junior electrician be permitted to take the vacation period given the junior maintenance pipe fitter. How would you expect an arbitrator to rule?

To Express One Thing Is to Exclude Another

To specifically include one item or class of items and not to mention others may be interpreted to mean that the others were intentionally *excluded.*

Example 1: "At the convenience of the company, swing-shift workers will be given 20 minutes from their regular shift to eat lunch."

Could straight day workers claim the same benefit?

Example 2: In a discipline clause calling for progressive discipline one sentence states: "Immediate discharge may be imposed for drunkenness, theft, or gross insubordination."

Could a company immediately discharge two employees for fighting at work? One employee for fighting with a supervisor?

Example 3: "In determining vacation eligibility, an employee's total service with the company at this or any other plant shall be used."

"All employees in the bargaining unit will accrue 15 days sick leave per year of service to a maximum of 190."

An employee who had 20 years service with the company, but only two years of service at the plant, put in a grievance for 190 days sick leave credit rather than the 30 granted him by the company. How would an arbitrator rule?

Enumeration Limits the General Language to the Category of the Enumerated Items

A list of specific items followed by more general language will limit the general language to items, examples, situations similar to those enumerated.

Example 1: "Seniority shall govern in all cases of layoff, promotion, transfer, and other adjustments of personnel."

"Overtime shall be shared among employees within a given classification."

How would an arbitrator rule on a demand by a senior electrician that he, rather than a junior electrician, should have been given a certain overtime assignment?

Example 2: "Coffee breaks, library privileges, gym privileges, free parking, and other existing benefits will continue unaltered for the duration of the agreement."

The employer seeks to change the daily schedule so that only half the secretarial employees are at lunch at any time. The union claims a violation of the above language. What do you think an arbitrator would rule?

Words Judged by Their Context

Where words appear often determines what was meant by their use.

Example 1: "Section 5: Holidays Worked"

"Holiday pay of eight hours plus time worked at the regular rate will be paid for holidays worked."

"Section 6: Holidays Not Worked"

"To be eligible for holiday pay an employee must work the scheduled day before and the scheduled day after the holiday."

An employee was absent the day before a holiday but worked eight hours on the holiday. The company paid him his regular pay but denied him holiday pay. As the union, how would you argue this case?

Example 2: If you were the company how would you argue this same case if the language read as follows:

"Section 4: Holidays"

"To be eligible for holiday pay an employee must work the scheduled day before and the scheduled day after the holiday."

"If an employee works on a holiday, he will be paid eight hours at his regular rate in addition to his eight hours of holiday pay."

Construing the Agreement as a Whole

A broader application of the same concept is reading not only the words but also the clauses and sections as a part of the total labor agreement.

Where one interpretation would give meaning to one section to the exclusion of other sections, and a second interpretation would give meaning to both sections, the broader interpretation would generally be followed. Arbitrators assume that the parties do not write meaningless provisions.

Example 1: "Overtime will be equalized within each classification. The employee at the end of the week with the least credited overtime will be given the first opportunity for overtime in the following work week."

"Every reasonable effort will be made to assign daily overtime contiguous to an employee's regular shift."

"The company will endeavor to avoid scheduling employees for more than twelve hours in any given twenty-four hour period. All time worked in excess of twelve hours will be paid at the double time rate."

John Smith was a forklift operator on the 8:00 A.M. to 4:00 P.M. shift and had the lowest accumulated overtime in the workweek ending Friday, June 10, 1977. The plant did not operate over the weekend. On the first shift on June

13, Bob Wilson, a forklift operator on the 4:00 P.M. to 12:00 midnight shift, who had more accumulated overtime than John, was called out to work four hours overtime from midnight until 4:00 A.M. John Smith was called out to work from 4:00 A.M. until 8:00 A.M., and then worked his regular shift. He filed a grievance arguing he should have been called to work from 12:00 midnight until 4:00 A.M. since he was the forklift operator with the least accumulated overtime. How would you argue this case if you were the company?

Example 2: "Article X Regular Vacation"

"(d) Vacation Payment: The employee's regular vacation wage will be his regular standard daily wage, including any regularly scheduled overtime, at the time his vacation is due as set forth below."

"(f) Time of Payment: The vacation payment shall be made on the last pay day immediately preceding the beginning of the vacation period."

"Article XI Graduated Vacation"

"(e) Time of payment: Graduated vacation payment shall be made the last day immediately preceding the beginning of the employee's graduated vacation."

"(f) Rate of Payment: Graduated vacation payment will be based on the employee's regular standard daily wage rate including any regularly scheduled overtime at the time his vacation payment is due, as provided in section (e) above, and shall include any applicable shift differentials."

The regular vacation period was from June 19 to July 1, 1977. Employees received pay on June 11 and June 25. John Wilson and Rich Vedas were scheduled for 42.5 hours a week from January 8 to March 30, 1977. They worked 37.5 hours per week from March 31 to May 31. From June 1 to June 10 they worked nine hours a day on eight scheduled days. From June 11 to June 18 they worked 7.5 hours per day and 37.5 hours for the week. The normal work day is 7.5 hours at straight time. All time over 7.5 hours per day is paid at time and a half. On June 11, John and Rich received vacation pay for two weeks at 37.5 hours per week. They both filed grievances claiming that vacation pay should have been paid for 45 hours per week with 7.5 hours paid at the overtime rate. The company denied the grievance. If you were the company representative, how would you argue this case? What would you contend if you were the union?

Normal as Opposed to Technical Usage

Words will be given their commonly accepted meanings unless it is shown that both parties intended a technical or uncommon definition.

Example 1: "Vacation pay will be paid in accordance with an employee's average annual earnings."

Sam Jones was a relief operator at $5.00 an hour for 1500 straight-time hours in the past year, and for an additional 500 straight-time hours he worked as a maintenance machinist's helper at $5.50 per hour. The company argues that he should be paid vacation pay at the rate of $5.00 per hour. As the union representative, what would you argue?

Example 2: "Vacation pay will be paid in accordance with each employee's regular hourly rate."

Under this contract language, how much should Sam get for 80 hours of vacation?

Example 3: Sam worked 2,000 hours straight-time at $7.50 per hour in the past year. Given the contract language in example 1, what should Sam be paid for 80 hours of vacation?

The above contract construction guidelines are not exhaustive and often overlap and even conflict with one another in a given case. They cannot be applied mechanically and must often be considered in conjunction with other guides such as "intent" and "past practice." However, the actual wording of the labor agreement is of such importance that all case preparations must begin with a careful study of that contract language.

Other Arguments

While contract language is, of course, the best evidence of what the parties intended, the written word is not always clear. Determining what was intended in negotiations may often require inquiry which goes beyond a mere study of the language. To conduct such an inquiry properly the company and union spokesmen need to be aware of other possible arguments and how they may, or may not, influence an arbitrator.

Establishing Intent

Notes, rough drafts, etc., particularly if initialed by both parties, can be very helpful. Even notes kept by one party, if supplemented by the testimony of a person present during those negotiations, may prove quite convincing to an arbitrator.

In most instances, companies seem to keep more complete and detailed notes on negotiations than do their union counterparts. There seems to be no very good reason for this, as the typical union bargaining committee usually has at least one and, more often, two or more members who have almost nothing to do but sit, listen, and take notes. Whether the company or union keeps poor records, the fact that such notes are not taken—or, if taken, are misplaced or lost—is simply a matter of poor collective bargaining practices.

The parties' various written proposals can also indicate intent. For example, if one party has submitted a change in the contract language but failed to obtain the other party's agreement, an arbitrator will consider this strong evidence that the existing language means something quite different from the language proposed in the rejected change. To illustrate, suppose (1) a union proposed that employees clearly have the right to exercise seniority in the choice of shifts, (2) the contract was ambiguous on the point, and (3) the company rejected the union's proposal. Subsequently, if the union attempted to grieve the denial of an employee's shift preference, the union would have a very weak case. In other words, if a company or union believes new language is necessary to resolve a matter in its favor, then the *old* language must not support its position.

On the other hand, when a contract *is* modified, one must assume that the old language and the old meaning no longer apply. Suppose an employer argues that any employee who fails to work a scheduled holiday forfeits both his holiday pay and his regular pay for that day. If it is shown that an old contract required employees to work a scheduled holiday or forfeit holiday pay, but the requirement has since been deleted in negotiations, an arbitrator would no doubt rule that there is no longer a holiday pay restriction.

In short, clear records of past negotiations can often prove extremely valuable in arguing the intent of existing contract language.

Fairness and Efficiency Considerations

It cannot be said too often that an arbitrator is *not* hired to impose his sense of equity on the parties. Nonetheless, if there are two possible interpretations of a clause, he will choose the one yielding the "fairest" result.

Example 1: "Any employee having six days of unexcused absences in six months will receive a written warning. If the employee has two more days of unexcused absence in the next six months, he will be discharged."

> The union in a case argued that the
> six-month period began with the first
> day of unexcused absence. At the end
> of that six-month period, an em-
> ployee's record should be wiped clean
> if he had not accrued six days of
> unexcused absence. According to the
> union, a new six-month term would
> begin with the employee's next day of
> unexcused absence. The union also
> submitted evidence that the company
> had followed the above practice for
> over a year. The company argued that
> the language should be interpreted to
> mean six days of unexcused absence
> in *any* six-month period, and that the
> record should be continuing. How
> would you expect an arbitrator to
> rule?

From a company standpoint the need for
"efficiency" is similar to a union's desire for
"fairness." Again an arbitrator may not substitute
his concept of the best "way to run a railroad" for
what the parties have agreed to. Still, language
permitting, arbitrators try to avoid awards that
will create inefficient work practices.

Example 2: "Supervisory employees shall perform no classified work covered by
this agreement except in emergencies
and except if such work is necessary
for the purpose of training or instruct-
ing classified employees."

The operation of the man hoist at a
certain coal mine was classified work,
and for safety reasons state law
required a trained and "certified"

hoist operator be present on top when anyone went below. The union contended that even on idle days when the mine did not operate, a certified, classified hoist operator (member of the bargaining unit) should have been present if only two employees went below. The company argued that as long as any certified hoist operator, even a supervisor, was present to cover emergencies, management did not need to call in classified hoist operators on idle days. How would you have argued this case as the company? The union?

Interpretations in Light of the Law

Although arbitrators are not hired to interpret law but only the labor agreement, it may occur that between two opinions, one is clearly illegal and the other legal. An arbitrator will, of course, choose a legal over an illegal interpretation. However, it is often much more complex than that. (See Chapter 7, "The Law and Arbitration.") Needless to say, the contract language is rarely so ambiguous and the law so clear that the choice is simple. More often than not these days, the law is substantially more difficult to understand than the contract.

Avoiding Penalties and Forfeitures

Unless the contract clearly stipulates a penalty award, arbitrators will attempt to construe a contract in a manner that does not penalize a party. Most commonly, this means that unions and employees can only expect to obtain a "make whole" award, and not a "bonus" or a "fine" against the company, even when the company has made an error.

Example 1: "Employees will share equally in weekend overtime work within their classification."

Harry Wilson had 250 hours of overtime credited to him as of Friday, June 10, 1977. Of five classified tractor operators, he had the least amount of credited overtime. Robert Gibbons, also a tractor operator, had 252 hours of credited overtime. The company scheduled him to work Sunday, June 12, 1977, for eight hours at double time. On June 13, Harry grieved, asking for eight hours pay at double-time rate. The company offered to give Harry the first call for Sunday overtime until such time as he would no longer be the low overtime man among the tractor operators. Harry insists he is entitled to the pay. How should the company argue this case?

Example 2: Suppose Gibbons were a classified shovel operator who was called out on Sunday and, instead of operating a shovel, performed tractor operator work. Given the contract language cited above, what would the union's argument be on behalf of Harry Wilson, low overtime man among the tractor operators?

Example 3: Howard Kawalski was fired for stealing copper tubing on May 5, 1978. He went to the union hall and was immediately referred out to work on highway construction. The union grieved the discharge. Before the case could come to arbitration another man admitted the theft on August 25, 1978, completely clearing Howard. The company apologized to Howard and offered him his old job back, but refused back pay, claiming that Howard had suffered no loss. The union claimed the company should disregard any outside earnings and pay Howard what he would have earned had he not been fired. How do you think an arbitrator would rule?

Avoiding Harsh or Nonsensical Results

Although a given clause may literally call for some nonsensical result, arbitrators will endeavor to find an alternate meaning which makes more sense or is less harsh.

Example 1: "All employees in the active employ of the company on June 1 of each year will receive vacation time based on their length of service and in proportion to their hours worked the previous year according to the following schedule...."

Sam Wilson, an employee of 10 years, was on sick leave the week of May 29–June 4. He had worked 2,500 hours the year of June 1, 1976, to June 1, 1977. Can he properly be denied vacation pay?

Example 2: "Employees shall be expected to maintain production in accordance with their past performance and their failure to do so may result in their transfer to a lower paid job."

Robert Hawkins was, for years, the outstanding screw-machine operator in his department. He regularly produced 25 percent more than the department average. However, due to advancing age and an increasing drinking problem, his production had fallen to the department average. The company sought to transfer Hawkins on the grounds that he had not maintained his past production. What do you think an arbitrator might have said in such a case?

Experience and Training of Negotiators

An arbitrator dealing with a contract written by parties unused to negotiating and drafting contracts may not feel as constrained by the language as he would when dealing with a contract drawn by skilled negotiators. Skilled negotiators can be expected to examine the language closely.

For example, a contract between small employers and certain unions may not have a specific requirement that discipline be only for "just cause." None of the small employers may ever raise an objection to cases grieved by the union on the basis of no "just cause." Even if they did object, however, it might be argued that given the informality and unsophisticated nature of their relationships, the "for just cause only" requirement was always assumed by such employers and their respective unions.

On the other hand, a contract, prepared by skilled negotiators, with the company's disciplinary powers outlined in great detail, but without a "just cause" clause, is not likely to be viewed by an arbitrator as a contract in which the lack of that clause is an oversight. Skilled negotiators do not leave out such language inadvertently.

Past Practice

Perhaps no term is more misused than that of "past practice." For a union representative, establishing that a past practice actually exists, and then persuading an arbitrator to make an award based on that past practice, is indeed a difficult set of tasks.

A past practice can be defined as a "uniform" response to a "recurring" situation over a "substantial" period of time when that response is known, or should be known, by "responsible" union and company representatives.

The "uniformity" of a given practice need not be without an exception or two. It must be so overwhelmingly consistent, however, as to leave no doubt that the parties have regularly handled a matter in an established way. The exceptions must be rare enough to be looked upon as unintended errors or departures from a rule. Plainly the more uniform the occurrence, the stronger the evidence of a past practice.

A recurring response is a response which obviously has occurred more than a few times, and not only under exceptional circumstances. The more often it has happened in the routine performance of work, the stronger the evidence of a "past practice."

Closely related to recurrence is the time period in which a practice has existed. Again, the longer the time period, the better one can argue that a past practice exists. When a practice exists across two contracts, that is, when it overlaps a renegotiation of the agreement, it strongly suggests to an arbitrator that the parties have accepted it. Both have had an opportunity to deal with it and have not done so.

The mutuality of a practice (its acceptance by both parties) cannot always be proven. It can, however, often be inferred from the uniformity, repetition, and duration discussed above. At some point, an arbitrator must conclude that any responsible union or company representative cannot possibly have ignored a matter, though one party may *claim* ignorance of its existence.

Ascertaining who are "responsible" union and company representatives is more difficult. A good rule of thumb might be: Place the responsibility for accepting a past practice with the same person (or position) who had responsibility for negotiating the written agreement. This insures that no practice can exist which defines, or redefines, the basic written understanding unless that practice has at least implicit recognition by those responsible for the written document. However, depending on the union and management structure, as well as the leeway in a given agreement, a lower level of management and labor may well be ruled sufficiently "responsible" to have "recognized" a given practice. For example, in coal mining, a practice at one mine may have meaning for that particular mine, but it need not extend to other mines. The overall contract is industrywide but allows considerable leeway for labor and management at the local level. Similarly, no practice in one department of a local plant can be extended to the whole plant unless it is clearly accepted by the union officers and management representatives who, respectively, head the local union and local plant. Moreover, an understanding *within* a department or a single shift is not usually binding on even that shift or department if it varies from other shifts or in other departments. To make such a practice binding, it must be clearly shown to arise from circumstances unique to that group of employees. It must also be recognized and accepted by higher union and management representatives.

Even when a past practice is shown to meet the above criteria, it may still not prove conclusive in a given case, since contract language takes precedence when there is a conflict between a practice and that language. Essentially, reliance on past practice can occur in three situations:

    a. Where the contract language is ambiguous.
    b. Where the contract is silent.
    c. Where the contract is clear.

In the case of ambiguous language, past practice is critical and in most cases, controlling. In essence, the parties have resolved any ambiguity by their actions. It may safely be said that their actions, "the practice," have interpreted what they believe the language means.

Of course, when a contract contains language which requires that an employer take certain actions in accordance with past practice, or states that the employer may not diminish established benefits, the language clearly establishes past practice as a part of the agreement.

When the contract is silent, there seems to be some agreement among many arbitrators that if it is a practice involving an employee "benefit" such as a dinner allowance, discount price for products, a Christmas turkey, etc., the practice has been accepted as the perquisite, so to speak, of employment. On the other hand, if it is a practice involving operating methods and direction of the work force, management still retains the right to alter its practices. Unfortunately, there may be a number of issues that do not clearly fall into either of these categories.

If the contract language is clear and unambiguous, the near unanimous opinion of arbitrators is that the language should control rather than a contrary past practice. However, evidence that the parties simply made an error in drawing up the contract language, or other evidence of mutual intent to continue the practice regardless of the language, could result in an arbitrator's upholding the practice in spite of the written contractual terms.

Discussion Problems on Past Practices

1. How should an arbitrator rule on the elimination of 15-minute coffee breaks in the morning and afternoon when that has been the clear past practice for years? The contract is silent.

2. A foreman, a steward, and employees in Department A, midnight shift, work out an arrangement whereby employees who produce a certain number of parts are permitted to go to the lunchroom and play cards. Employees in Department B discover this practice and file a grievance requesting the same treatment. The contract is silent except for a section stating the hours of the three shifts. How would you expect an arbitrator to rule on such a grievance?

3. In the same case, the company eliminates the above practice in Department A. The steward files a grievance. Would an arbitrator be likely to support that grievance?

4. The contract states that the "company will provide all required safety equipment." When the company had required employees to wear safety equipment in the past, the company and employees had each paid a portion of the cost, depending on the anticipated private use. On safety shoes, for example, the company paid half and the employees half. On prescription safety glasses, the company paid 40 percent and employees paid 60 percent. After the passage of OSHA, the company required all employees to have safety hard hats and charged each employee for half the cost. If you were the union how would you argue this case?

5. For six years a utility company had a policy of providing box lunches or reimbursement of dinner money when a line crew was held overtime to make repairs. The contract was silent on this matter and further stated that the contract constituted the full and complete agreement between the union and company. The company failed to deliver box lunches to employees on the Havana line crew on Friday night, June 19, 1977, and subsequently refused to reimburse the men for steak dinners at the El Rancho Supper Club. The union grieved. If you were the company, how would you defend your position?

6. In the maintenance section, it was the company's practice to keep a skilled employee and his laborer helper overtime when working on equipment repair. On June 8, 1977, however, the company kept Millwright Smith over to continue repairing a

molder machine but told Jones, his helper and a first shift laborer, to punch out. The company assigned a second shift laborer from the labor pool, Hawkins, to assist Smith. Jones filed a grievance demanding "the overtime work done by Hawkins." The contract job description places all laborers in the same general classification. How would you guess an arbitrator would rule?

7. The first and second one-year contracts between a government agency and its public employees had a provision stating "existing benefits will not be diminished for the life of the agreement." The employer had initially provided free parking at its temporary facilities. When it moved to a new building, still under construction, it also had a free parking area. In negotiations for a first contract the union asked for contract language guaranteeing a number of specific benefits, including free parking. The employer refused to include free parking and certain other benefits in the contract but ultimately agreed to the language quoted above. Employees continued to park for free throughout the first year of the agreement.

In negotiations for the second contract, the matter of free parking was not raised by either party and the same "existing benefits" language was put into the agreement. Within a month after it was signed, a notice was sent to all employees explaining that gates would be put up at each parking area. There would be a $40-a-year charge for employees using the lots. The union filed a grievance, and the matter was brought to arbitration. How would you argue the case as either the union, or the employer?

8. The local contract states: "Overtime opportunities will be shared fairly among employees within each department." For six years, in Department C, the steward and the foreman have agreed to give the more senior employees first opportunity at all overtime. In ten other departments and in the maintenance crew, overtime is shared on an equalized basis. The senior employees filed a grievance in Department D demanding first opportunity at all overtime. If you were an arbitrator, how would you rule?

The company orders Department C to divide overtime opportunities equally among the employees in that department. The steward files a grievance alleging a violation of contract and past practice. Again, how would you rule?

Evidence

Until now, we have focused on interpretation of the labor agreement by first applying the rules of contract construction and then considering external factors which most often have a bearing on the written agreement. Evidence (the labor agreement itself; written contract proposals; testimony of witnesses about negotiations and past practices) is crucial in establishing interpretation and winning a case.

Most arbitration cases, however, also involve obtaining evidence about the events which gave rise to the grievance. On the whole, the facts of the occurrence and the facts which establish the meaning of the contract are unrelated; but one must obtain both to thoroughly prepare a case.

It may happen that the meaning or interpretation of the contract is not in dispute, and the sole controversy is over what occurred. On the other hand, the events giving rise to the dispute may be agreed upon, and the contract interpretation and application are the sole subject of controversy. In that event the facts establishing the meaning of the agreement are the crucial evidence. Most commonly, however, the parties cannot agree to either the contract interpretation or the events.

If the grievance procedure is operating correctly, both the union and company should have a clear idea of what is in dispute when they decide to go to arbitration. In order to simplify their preparation, ideally they should sit together and discuss what they agree upon and what is still in controversy. One party should, however, never assume that the other party agrees to a matter unless that agreement is made very clear. If one of the adversaries is later unable to furnish evidence on a point because it assumed there was agreement, it will be too late, in most instances, to remedy the situation.

In all instances, preparation of a case should commence with the contract language—even if the meaning of the language is not in dispute. The contract is the basis of the arbitrator's authority to make any ruling. If the disputants jointly stipulate to the contract meaning, they are free to spend more time establishing their respective versions of events. This simplifies both their tasks and the arbitrator's.

The following is a step-by-step outline which may prove helpful in case preparation:

1. Assuming there is argument over language implementation, start with the contract.
   a. Write out or outline all contract provisions, or parts of provisions, that support your interpretation.
   b. Using the rules of contract construction, write out your interpretation(s). Use as many words and phrases from the contract as possible.
   c. Apply any relevant arguments based on equity, common sense, and past practice that will help support your contract interpretation.
   d. Assemble the facts and evidence needed to support the assertions made in a, b, and c above. For example:
      (1) Have the contract ready as joint exhibit 1.
      (2) List any supporting facts that the other side will agree to.
      (3) Review previous contracts or written contract proposals, resolved grievances, and other arbitration awards.
      (4) Screen witnesses who can testify directly to the meaning the parties gave the language during negotiations and grievance meetings.
   e. Next, do all the above as if you were the other side. Stop—go back and do *all* of the above as if you were your opposite number!
   f. Review all of the opposing arguments and evidence you anticipate and write out a response that either:
      (1) refutes that argument or evidence, or
      (2) minimizes or diminishes its importance.
2. Assuming there is some dispute as to the oc-

currence that caused the grievance, follow these steps:

a. Write out a clear chronological sequence of events noting the dates and times, the main participants and any witnesses, the exact locations of events. In short, describe what happened in detail.

b. See what the other side agrees with. If *both* of you can agree on a matter, label it a *fact*.

c. List documents and witnesses that will confirm the above rendition of events.

d. Prepare an explanation of events: Why did one event follow another? Why was Sam angry? Why did the foreman send Sam home?

e. Explain why your version of what happened establishes that the company did or did not violate the contract.

f. Next, do all the above as if you were working for your opponent. Then, prepare to rebut or diminish that position.

3. Prepare your evidence for presentation.

a. See if you can obtain a signed, written stipulation of facts. If not, find out what differences there are.

b. Prepare a copy of all your documents in triplicate—normally Xeroxing is the quickest and cheapest method.

(1) Obtaining copies of your own documents should not be difficult; however, the other party may have documents and records (e.g., absentee records) which are critical to your case. Most commonly the employer has many more personnel records than does the union. If you want a given record, first make an oral request and explain its necessity in assessing the

merits of the grievance. If the other party refuses to cooperate, submit the request in writing. If you are under the National Labor Relations Act, and your adversary again refuses, file a charge with the nearest NLRB office. Also keep a copy of the request to show the arbitrator at the hearing if you have still not obtained the information. Under either state or national labor law, the parties are entitled to information needed to intelligently process a grievance. But even if you are not covered by such law, the arbitrator should give a sympathetic hearing to any reasonable request for information.

(2) In order to establish their authenticity, some documents, such as notes taken in bargaining or at a grievance meeting or the daily log kept by a steward or a foreman, will probably require testimony from the individual who kept the record.

c. Decide who your witnesses will be and who will probably testify for the other party. Keep in mind the following:

(1) It is better to have no witness than a witness with a weak grip on the truth. Whenever one of your witnesses is shown to be lying, it raises a question about the testimony of all your witnesses.

(2) Many people are "tigers" in a bar, company offices, or the union hall, but unless a witness can stand up to tough cross-examination, you may want to reconsider his use.

(3) Do *not* tell your people what to say, but *do* go over your questions with them and

know the general nature of their responses. Have a colleague ask them the questions they can expect from your adversary. This should be done in a tough no-holds-barred fashion. To be effective, a witness should know what to expect.

Urge your witnesses to stay calm and unexcited. Warn them not to argue, but to answer honestly to the best of their ability. Explain that their role is to testify to what they know, and that they are not on the stand to plead the case.

(4) Consider the other party's choice of witnesses, and request a list ahead of time. Be prepared to exchange your list for theirs unless, of course, you believe that they may intimidate your witnesses.

(5) Consider carefully whether you wish to call union or management members who may know something concerning the contract or events that would prove helpful, even though they may not be sympathetic to your position. In the course of the grievance procedure, you should inform the other party of your intention to call these witnesses, and should try to obtain some idea of their testimony. Don't wait until the day of the hearing to ask the other side to produce a witness with whom you've had no discussion. To do so not only smacks of "sand-bagging," but may also produce some testimony that you do not want to hear.

(6) Anticipate what adverse witnesses will say, and be prepared to cross-examine them.

(7) Be prepared to challenge and undercut

crucial hostile testimony. The *best* way to accomplish this is to find contradictions or inconsistencies in an individual's testimony or between the statements of different adverse witnesses. However, the mere fact that a contradiction exists between the testimony of union and company witnesses is to be expected and will not necessarily discredit either. But, pointing out that an opposing witness has contradicted himself in matters of time, place, or personnel may be the simplest way to demonstrate his lack of credibility to the arbitrator. Contradictions in testimony from different hostile witnesses will also prove helpful, but may simply be due to differences of perception and memory. Actually, when two or more witnesses give *exactly* the same version of events, one wonders whether it is true recall or merely the memorized repetition of some prearranged version of events. Remember also that precise recollection of events several months old is unusual unless there were some particular reasons that a person remarked the events at the time. Be wary of testimony that recreates the details of events with great precision.

Finding inconsistencies in testimony, and exploiting those inconsistencies, requires experience as well as a sensitive ear and a quick mind and pencil. If you anticipate major questions of credibility within the other party's testimony or between the testimony of the two sides, have someone assist you in keeping track of, and noting, inconsistencies. You, however, should remain the spokesman.

Also, remember that most people do not lie but rather slant the truth. Be ready to explain to the arbitrator any reason a hostile witness might have for "slanting."

(8) Even though you are presenting the case, you may also testify. Of course you then must be ready to submit to cross-examination.

(9) Do not feel required to call witnesses. If you can establish a fact without the use of witnesses, do so. You never know for sure what people will say when they testify.

If for political and/or educational reasons you wish to bring a large number of people to the hearing, don't box yourself into having to use them in some way. Just explain to the other side and the arbitrator that you want such people present in order to give them a better understanding of the grievance and arbitral process. Of course, the employer may draw the line if such a large attendance is interfering with production. Moreover, whoever calls employees to such hearings must usually pay for their lost time.

Never bring a large crowd for the purpose of attempting to intimidate witnesses and/or the arbitrator.

(10) From time to time the company and/or the union may request the sequestering of witnesses. The purpose is to insure

that one witness will not hear another's testimony and then alter his own accordingly. As long as you instruct your people to tell the truth to the best of their knowledge, you should never feel threatened by the practice of sequestering witnesses.

Note, though, that in discipline and discharge cases the grievant is normally permitted to remain, on the theory that he should hear all the evidence and testimony against him.

(11) Instruct your people on proper conduct during the hearing. You may find it necessary to make clear ahead of time that you don't want a constant flow of notes from assistants or witnesses interrupting your train of thought and questioning. If you anticipate any problem, let your people know that you will caucus from time to time so they may air their views privately.

Warn those accompanying you that vocal, facial, and other demonstrations do not help your case; i.e., people who groan, snicker, shake their heads, etc., when opposing witnesses are testifying may suggest that this is your only way of rebutting the testimony. Remember, too, that union and company people have to go on working with one another for a long time after the arbitration case is over.

(12) Do not plan to attack a witness's background, character, life-style, drinking habits, intelligence, etc., unless this clearly has bearing on the case. Embar-

rassing a witness for the sake of his embarrassment is not only churlish and unconstructive, but also makes you look either stupid or small in the eyes of most arbitrators. Either a personal matter *obviously* has something to do with a case, or it should *not* be raised.

Remedies

In the course of filing the grievance and processing the matter to arbitration, you will already have given some thought to the remedy claimed. However, assuming the case may go against the employer, you may want to spend some time prior to the hearing defining exactly what is an appropriate remedy. Normally, the remedy requested is a "make whole" remedy; that is, the individual or group of employees will recover any loss they have incurred. Unfortunately, the full extent of losses is often unclear until after an award. A union should be prepared, though, to indicate to the arbitrator the losses it anticipates, and the company, of course, should be prepared to give its version of those losses. The following are some questions you may wish to ask yourself when anticipating a proper remedy.

Union: Aside from wages, what else did the employee lose?

Did a discharged employee incur medical expenses that would have been covered by his insurance policy?

Did he lose any paid vacation, or holiday?

Did he miss out on any promotion opportunities?

Assuming he is made whole for his lost

wages, how much has inflation affected the purchasing power of this money?

Company: Did the employee have other work and what was he paid?
Did the employee receive unemployment benefits, workmen's compensation benefits?
Did the employee turn down offers of employment?

Both: Can you agree on an exact dollar figure for his loss?
Does the employee agree that this figure is correct?

The standard advice for unions is to ask for money plus any necessary corrective action such as reinstatement, promotion, ordering the foreman to cease doing bargaining unit work, etc. This advice is based on the quite sensible belief that most employees will find some use for such a remedy and, also, that the way to an employer's heart is through his pocketbook. It is assumed that behavior which costs money will be corrected and not repeated. If an employer has only to correct his actions at no cost, he will have little incentive to change practices. This, however, does not alter the principle that arbitrators will not support penalties or forfeitures unless clearly called for by the agreement. It simply means that "make whole" remedies often involve costs which would not have occurred had the contract been followed more closely.

The parties should always attempt to obtain a clear or exact remedy from an arbitrator. If that is impossible, they should insure that the arbitrator retains jurisdiction to subsequently award a precise remedy, should the union and company be unable to agree. It makes little sense to go to arbitration twice for one award.

A clear remedy also has the advantage of informing the grievant(s) of what can be expected if the union prevails completely. It does no one any good if grievants still feel aggrieved after receiving an award. It is best to make clear to the grievant(s) the possible outcomes in a given case and it is unwise to encourage false expectations.

Preparing an Opening Statement

Having completed the above case preparation, you may now wish to write an opening statement which should introduce the arbitrator to the case and, if possible, get him thinking in your terms. An opening statement is *not* evidence and anything asserted in that statement should subsequently be proven. Such a statement serves two purposes: to cite and explain the contract provisions, if any, you believe are controlling and to describe your version of relevant events. Allow the arbitrator time to look at, and read, the provisions cited. You may even want to read the most relevant contract provisions aloud. Give him time to hear, absorb, write down, and understand your description of what happened. Remember, it is unlikely that he has ever seen your contract or worksite before, and he is certainly unfamiliar with the specific events of your case. Take time to explain your case to him right from the start. You may want to present the arbitrator with a written copy of your opening statement so that he will have it available for reference during the hearing and, later, when considering his decision. Of course, if the arbitrator receives a copy, courtesy demands that you also present a copy to your adversary.

6
Presenting the Case

Many labor and management people are under the impression that presentation is the key to successful arbitration cases. This error often costs them considerable sums of money as well as the loss of certain cases. Their misconception undoubtedly arises from an overdose of Perry Mason and Owen Marshall. Courtroom drama, a fine vehicle for selling toothpaste and other consumer products, is of little value in winning arbitration cases. If a case is good, and you are well prepared, the presentation can make little difference. If the case is bad, or you are ill-prepared, the presentation cannot correct the matter. Unlike a jury, an arbitrator is expected to have the expertise and opportunity to get at the essence of a case. He will normally be unimpressed with longwinded speeches and melodramatic examination or cross-examination of witnesses. This kind of posturing is more often designed to convince a client or members that the representative is doing his job than to convince the arbitrator of the merit of his case.

Instead of viewing the arbitration hearing as an arena for jousting and declaiming great sentiments, consider it a chance to place all the evidence and arguments before the arbitrator in an orderly fashion.

Procedures

Prior to the hearing, an ad hoc arbitrator will probably check your arbitration provision to inform himself of the extent of his authority and any peculiar procedural requirements. Permanent umpires will normally be conversant with the contract and will find this unnecessary.

The arbitrator may also inquire whether there are any procedural or substantive arbitrability questions. If such questions are raised, he will attempt to find a mutually agreeable way of resolving them prior to hearing the merits of the grievance. Of course, it may occur (as indicated in Chapter 3) that such a question *must* be decided before the merits can be heard. If no such questions arise, he may then outline his method of conducting a hearing. If the arbitrator fails to state his procedure; if you do not understand it; or if you differ with him; the time to raise questions or objections is at the outset. Certainly do not be embarrassed to inquire or disagree, but do resist being surly or unnecessarily argumentative. Above all, be sure you know when you are to present your case. Otherwise you could stumble through the hearing without ever giving the arbitrator all your evidence and arguments.

Although procedures may vary somewhat, arbitrators typically give both parties an opportunity to make opening statements. When the union brings the grievance, it will be considered the moving party and will make the first statement.

When the company has discharged or disciplined an employee, it usually goes first and acts as the moving party.

If you have not initiated the case, you may decide to waive an opening statement until the other side has presented evidence. This is sometimes advantageous to the union in discipline cases when the full extent of the company's evidence against the employee is unknown. Ideally, of course, all this evidence should have been hashed out in the grievance procedure, but that, unfortunately, does not always happen. It makes little sense to waive an opening statement, however, if you are the first to present evidence. Without such a statement, the arbitrator has no idea what you are trying to prove with your evidence.

Do not be disturbed if your adversary waives an opening statement. This may only mean that the representative can't remember exactly what the case involves and is waiting for you to refresh his memory. His people may think he is engaging in deep strategy, but it shouldn't worry you. It means that the arbitrator will hear your evidence without any of the mental reservations your opponent could have instilled with an opening statement. Of course you run the same risk should you decline to make an opening statement.

After the opening statements the arbitrator may attempt to obtain a stipulation of the issue and any "facts" on which both parties agree.

The Issue

Some considerable care and caution is necessary when framing the issue. From a union standpoint, it should be neither so broad a claim that the contract and evidence cannot support it, nor so narrowly drawn that the union is tied to a very limited piece of language. For example, it would be better to claim an individual has been wronged on a given date, time, and place than to assert that senior employees have been systematically discriminated against. On the other hand, most managements prefer the narrowly drawn issue which asks: "Did the Company violate Article VIII Section 1 subparagraph (c) in assigning Bill Jones the job of elevator operator on April 8, 1977?" This turns the issue on a very narrow portion of the agreement and restricts the union from using the whole contract to sustain its claim. The parties should also clarify their wish that the arbitrator include the question of remedy as a part of the issue. This can be handled by insisting that the question, "If so, what should be the remedy?" be added following the statement of the main issue.

Some further examples may help. Pick the preferable issue from the union's (u), company's (c), and arbitrator's (a) point of view.

Example 1: Under a contract calling for "discipline only for just cause":

_____ Did the company unjustly discipline Tom Lester?

_____ Was Tom Lester unjustly discharged on April 8, 1977?

_____ May an employee refuse an order?

_____ Can the company discipline for insubordination?

_____ Was Tom Lester discharged for just cause?

_____ Was Tom Lester discharged for just cause on April 8, 1977, based on the evidence and reasons given at that time?

Example 2: Under a contract requiring the assignment of overtime on an equalized basis:

___Has the company violated the equalized overtime provision?

___Did the company properly assign overtime to Sam Smith on June 20, 1977?

___Does the low man on overtime always have first right to weekend overtime?

___Did the company violate the agreement when it failed to call Ralph Jones for overtime on June 19, 1977?

___What must the company do to properly assign overtime?

Example 3: Under a contract which requires the company to "promote the senior man, provided he is able to perform work":

___Was the company's promotion of Lonney Wilkins rather than Ben Crayshaw in good faith?

___Did the company properly deny Ben Crayshaw the promotion to Mechanic III?

___Is Ben Crayshaw able to perform the work of Mechanic III?

___Did the company violate the agreement when it awarded the position of Mechanic III to Lonney Wilkins rather than to Ben Crayshaw?

___Must the senior employee be promoted over the junior employee in all cases?

_____ Has the company been fair to Ben Crayshaw?

Rules of Evidence

After the opening statement and stipulation of the issue, if possible, the party bringing the case proceeds with its presentation of evidence. Arbitration hearings are quite informal compared with court proceedings, and the rules of evidence are not always followed strictly. In this area an excellent guide, strongly recommended for all practitioners, is Boaz Siegel's brief, handy book, *Proving Your Arbitration Case.** At the risk of being redundant with that fine book, the following are some guides to common problems encountered with rules of evidence.

a. Laymen are often flabbergasted by objections couched in technical legal language or Latin phrases. Don't hesitate to say you don't know what somebody is talking about—including the arbitrator. There is no legal objection or rule of evidence that cannot be explained in a commonsense way. If it cannot be thus explained, it probably lacks merit.

b. Representatives often tend to "lead" their own witnesses by making statements and simply asking the witness to agree or disagree. Many arbitrators will uphold an objection to "leading" because they want to hear what the witness has to say—not what you want him to agree or disagree with. To avoid leading your witnesses, ask straightforward questions and encourage them to tell it in their own words. When cross-

---

*Boaz Siegel, *Proving Your Arbitration Case* (Washington DC: BNA Books, 1961).

examining hostile witnesses you can, however, and often should, use leading questions. It's your job to expose any contradictions in your adversary's evidence.

c. Nonlawyers, also, often fail to "lay a foundation" for evidence. This is simply the task of establishing where a document came from, how a witness had knowledge of a matter, and so forth. In short, for some evidence to be meaningful, there must be some demonstration of its origin and even its authenticity.

d. Another problem is the tendency of witnesses to express their opinions rather than their observations. If you are trying to establish that a man had been drinking heavily, your witness's opinion that "Sam was drunk" is not nearly so convincing as testimony that he, the witness, observed that "Sam staggered; he slurred when he spoke to me; Sam's eyes were red; he cursed often and profusely," etc.

In this regard, it is also pointless to continually ask union or company witnesses what the contract states and to go over their opinions of language interpretation. You are in arbitration because you cannot agree on what the contract means. Having your witnesses concur with your interpretation, or forcing opposing witnesses to read aloud from the agreement, convinces an arbitrator of nothing.

If a witness is giving an opinon based on personal expertise, a foundation for that expertise should be laid. A doctor offering medical testimony or opinion should be properly introduced; a tool and die maker giving his opinion on tolerances in certain work should also be shown to command specialized knowledge. Without proper foundation, Joe Drake's opinion carries no more weight than any other witness's testimony.

e. The most common objection in arbitration hearings is to irrelevancy. These objections are most often made, not in the hope that the arbitrator will sustain the objection, but rather in an effort to minimize the importance of the evidence. Unless a matter is completely far-fetched or appears to be submitted for some ulterior purpose (such as blackguarding a foreman's character or intimidating a union witness) most arbitrators admit evidence "for what it's worth." Be prepared, however, to explain why you believe a given piece of testimony is relevant or irrelevant. Don't make an objection just because evidence is damaging, and don't pursue evidence which the arbitrator plainly indicates is irrelevant— unless, of course, you can adequately explain its relevancy.

f. Object strenuously to any effort by the other side to introduce evidence showing that you offered to "compromise" the case prior to the hearing. Such offers to compromise should never be allowed into evidence, because they may very likely prejudice the arbitrator. If one party is allowed to get a compromise offer before an arbitrator, both parties will thereafter be unwilling to compromise cases during the grievance procedure. This is obviously not a desirable situation, and arbitrators should be on their toes to prevent such evidence from creeping in.

Closing Statements, Briefs, and Transcripts

Most hearings could end with the parties' closing statements, thus eliminating the added step of post-hearing briefs. There are, however, a number of influences which, singly or in combination, prevent the parties from doing this.

Most attorneys like to file briefs and their clients often expect it. Some arbitrators like a brief to remind them of details in a case and to postpone the date when they must write a decision. Companies sometimes want a post-hearing brief because a brief delays the date when the company has to change its practices—assuming that it violated the agreement. And unions must want post-hearing briefs, because they have done very little to prevent the growth of this practice.

Unfortunately, often unions and sometimes companies feel pressured to submit a brief—particularly if the other party does. They fear, possibly with some justification, that an arbitrator may view failure to do so as an indication that they feel their own case lacks merit. Then, too, some representatives feel that their associates expect them to keep up with the other side. They are concerned that, by not filing, they will appear lazy.

Actually there is very little real justification for written post-hearing statements. Occasionally, a case may be so complex that both parties need some time to fully prepare their arguments after listening to all the evidence during the hearing. But, if the grievance procedure is working properly, each side should have been aware of the other's evidence and arguments before the hearing.

As stated in a previous discussion on arbitration clauses, perhaps the only way a party can protect itself from filing unnecessary briefs is to negotiate contract language requiring mutual agreement for such actions.

In any event, whether you must make a closing statement or write a post-hearing brief or both, the basic elements of such "concluding remarks" are the same. A closing statement or brief should summarize the relevant facts from your point of view and cogently argue that your interpretation of the contract and version of the facts are correct. You may also take this opportunity to rebut your opponent's contractual interpretation and rendition of events. Special care should be taken, however, in a closing statement or a brief not to assert any "fact" not placed in evidence at the hearing.

A clear record of a hearing is obviously desirable when there are substantial questions of fact. If the parties and the arbitrator all choose to use cassette tape recorders, a record can be made that, for clarity and completeness, is generally superior to a written transcript. This approach is inexpensive and expeditious but unfortunately has not obtained widespread acceptance by the parties and arbitrators.

Consequently, when a record is requested one must normally expect a delay while the transcript is prepared, a further delay while it is studied, and still another delay for filing of briefs. "Why have a transcript if you don't want to file a brief?" some will inquire. Yes, why indeed should court reporters be the only ones to profit from this delay? Again, the best way of eliminating this bother is to state in the labor agreement that transcripts may be made only with the written consent of both parties. With such language, however, one must expect to share in the cost of any transcript to which one agrees.

When the contract is silent on transcripts, one party may still decline to share in the expense of a transcript ordered by the other party. Furthermore, according to *The Code of Professional Responsibility for Arbitrators of Labor Management Disputes*, "the arbitrator may also make appropriate arrangements under which the other party may have access to a copy, if a copy is provided to the arbitrator."* Just how this is supposed to be done, unfortunately, is not explained in the Code.

---

*Page 19 of the Code: Labor and management representatives may wish to obtain a copy of this Code, although its practical use is somewhat limited. Having been prepared by experts on contract language, it is filled with discretionary terms. It does, however, occasionally come down hard on some things, e.g., arbitrators charging for time not spent on a case! or "An arbitrator must not permit personal relationships to affect decision making."

7

The Law and Arbitration

There is neither the space nor the need in a manual of this type to cover all ramifications of law and the arbitral process. Questions of substantive and procedural arbitrability have already appeared in Chapter 3. The following is an effort to summarize very briefly the grievance and arbitration relationship with the legal duty to represent all employees fairly, the law and/or the terms of an agreement, the legal status of swearing and subpoenaing witnesses in arbitration cases, and the NLRB's "policy" of deferral to arbitration.

Duty of Fair Representation

Under the National Labor Relations Act a union is legally obligated to represent employees fairly and may not discriminate against any employee for invidious reasons such as race, creed, color, union activity, etc. This means that a union should handle each grievance on its merits. It must be sure when dropping a grievance that it is not due to animosity towards the grievant(s). For example, a union may drop a grievance for tactical reasons or because of financial limitations. It is on unsafe ground, however, when it turns down a grievance because "Sam (the grievant) is a trouble-maker."

One appellate court ruled that a union was legally obligated to meet the established time limits in the grievance procedure even though the failure was not due to "bad faith." This, however, is quite unusual. The great bulk of court opinion has held that a union must be shown to have acted in bad faith before it can be held liable for any failure to effectively represent employees.

In addition to merely representing employees and processing their grievances, a union is under some legal obligation to dig out the facts in a case. Legality aside, the union should, as a practical matter, do its best to discover the facts and obtain all the evidence. Of course, there is a commonsense limit to investigation beyond which no one can expect a union to go. The courts on the whole understand this, and will, one hopes, eventually render decisions that clearly accept this fact of life.

Interpretation in Light of the Law

A different kind of legal problem arises when the arbitrator is urged to use law as the basis for his decision. There would appear to be a number of ways the "law" can be argued as a basis for a decision. The following four categories are an effort to distinguish among these various arguments.

1. When the contract is ambiguous, one party may urge that a given interpretation is in

compliance or conformity with the law, whereas another interpretation is not. The difficulty for most arbitrators is that this requires considerable knowledge of what the law says and means. Often the law itself is ambiguous, or contradictory court rulings exist. On the other hand, where the law is reasonably clear *and* the language is ambiguous, arbitrators would rather render a decision which will not be subject to a court challenge.

2. At times a contract will incorporate a law into the agreement. For example, a teacher-school-board agreement that calls for review of tenure decisions "in accordance with the State Public Education Code" has introduced the interpretation of that code into any arbitral review of a tenure decision.

3. Then again, the inclusion of law may simply be language which incorporates an essentially legal concept. For example, a contract which requires "non-discrimination" may well result in a hearing at which the parties introduce statutory language and court decisions based on the Equal Employment Opportunity Act. And a contract requiring "due process" in discipline cases should prove a godsend to some lawyer.

   On the whole, arbitrators are reluctant to stray far beyond the terms of the actual agreement, although legal language suggests "legal concepts" which an arbitrator may consider in reaching his decision.

4. Then there are cases in which one party claims that the other is doing something

illegal, or that the contract requires an illegal action. For example, a union might complain that the employer's actions violated the constitutional right to free speech. In another, a company could claim that a scheduled cost-of-living increase violated the Government's economic plan. Most arbitrators regard such questions as beyond their authority and appropriate for other forums: the federal courts or the council on wages and prices, respectively, in the above examples.

Legal Authority of Arbitrators

Arbitrators' legal powers depend upon the particular state and/or federal statute under which they operate. However, under the Uniform Arbitration Code, which is usually controlling, an arbitrator can swear witnesses, issue subpoenas, conduct *ex parte* hearings, and, most important, make final and binding decisions when that is called for in the contract. Arbitrators have no great problem swearing in witnesses or writing binding decisions; however, some arbitrators will be uncomfortable issuing subpoenas and most attempt to avoid conducting *ex parte* hearings. Arbitrators tend to view labor arbitration as a process requiring mutual consent. Since they are selected by both parties, they are unwilling to alienate one party by forcing appearances or conducting hearings without that party's cooperation.

NLRB Deferral to Arbitration

As a result of recent changes (1977) in Board policy, the Board and arbitration are essentially back to the *Collyer* decision. This, in essence, means that if the union contends some management action is a violation of the legal duty to bargain, and a grievance and arbitration procedure exists, the Board will defer to arbitration. However, the ongoing saga of the NLRB and arbitration isn't over yet; so watch for new developments.

Plainly the above subjects are much more complex than these brief summaries would suggest. Why else should lawyers be kept on retainer? However, the above materials should assist the parties in knowing when to consult an attorney. On the whole it should be a rare grievance that requires expert legal advice on these or any other matters.

8

The Award

Under the AAA and FMCS guidelines an arbitrator has 30 and 60 days, respectively, to render his decision. The days are measured from the date of hearing or the date of receipt of the last communication (transcript or brief). Any requests by the arbitrator for time extensions should be made to both litigants. Parties often grumble that the time limit is not being met, yet are hesitant to complain while the decision is pending for fear of prejudicing their case. If you feel there has been unwarranted delay in the rendering of an award, you should so inform the appointing agency and the arbitrator after the award is received. Until more parties do complain, these delays can be expected to continue and possibly grow even longer.

Parties often skip to the last page of a decision to quickly discover the outcome. Later, representatives would be well advised to read the entire decision carefully. This will not only fully familiarize them with the specific award's application to the given grievance, but will also aid in teaching them how arbitrators reason and on what their decisions are based.

A file might be kept of awards according to subject matter. If your organization has a sufficient number of cases to justify the clerical work, awards can also be classified by arbitrator. The first set of records enables the ready identification of all awards that affect the various provisions of the contract. The latter permits familiarity with a given arbitrator's reasoning, prejudices, and predilections.

The main purpose of an award is to assist the parties by resolving the specific dispute and clarifying the agreement for future cases. Thus, when another grievance arises on the same matter, the parties will be able to resolve the dispute long before it reaches the final step of the grievance procedure. And that, of course, is the function of arbitration: to resolve the given controversy and, one way or the other, to end grievances arising from that controversy.

It is hoped that this manual will assist in the resolution of grievances without the need to proceed to arbitration. Certainly the careful selection and preparation of cases for arbitration will discourage violations of the agreement and frivolous grievances and will increase the chances for disputes being resolved in the grievance procedure.

Until another grievance arises, the arbitrator's award is the last phase of the procedure and the final subject of this manual; the thoughtful study of that award can be considered "preparation"— for the next case.

Arbitration Case Analysis Form
(Use one to prepare your case and
another to prepare your adversary's)

Location _____ Case # _____

Statement of Issues or Grievance: _____

_____

Relevant Contract Clauses: _____

_____

Interpretations of Clauses: _____

_____

_____

_____

_____

_____

Contractual Matters Not in Dispute: _____

_____

Contractual Matters in Dispute: _____

_____

_____

_____

_____

Evidence Supporting Contract Language (contract,
grievances, previous arbitration awards, old contracts, contract proposals; past practice(s), letters
of understanding; company rules, policies, procedures; participants in negotiations, etc.):

1. Documents: _____

_____

2. Witnesses: _____

_____

Anticipated Rebuttal: _____

_____

Incident(s) or Event(s) Giving Rise to the Grievance (describe in chronological order, specifically
noting who, what, when, where, and why):

_____

_____

_____

_____

_____

_____

_____

Facts Not in Dispute: _____

_____

_____

Facts in Dispute: _____

_____

_____

_____

_____

_____

Evidence to Support the Description of Events:
1. Documents: _____

_____

2. Witness: _____

_____

Anticipated Rebuttal: _____

_____